HOW TO MANAGE A TEAM LIKE A DECENT AND REASONABLE HUMAN BEING

YOU CAN BECOME A GREAT LEADER JUST BY
NOT BEING A D!CK

BRUCE WOLF

WOLF MOUNTAIN
– PUBLISHING –

Dedicated to the leaders who have shown me what it means to manage like a decent and reasonable human being.

CONTENTS

FOREWORD

Don't be a dick.

That's the kind of language I use in this book.

If that offends you, I'm not sorry.

Maybe you never watched cable television or went to middle school to become desensitized to this sort of unmannerly language, but if you can't handle it, you should probably put this book back on the shelf or hit the back button on your browser.

Everyone communicates in different ways and I just can't express the ideas in this book without words like that. It's how I'm wired.

If that doesn't work for you, no hard feelings. Good luck with Mary Poppins Management or whatever leadership-book-of-the-month with no potty words you're going to read next.

Bye.

Ok, for those of you that are still here, welcome. I probably won't say very many other bad words here (though you might catch a "damn" or even a few "ass"es), but I will talk straight and if you can't handle a 2nd grade swear word, you probably won't want to hear it.

Leading with "Don't be a dick" is my way of avoiding a bunch of pearl-clutching one-star reviews from people who buy this and get surprised halfway through.

It's also the entire premise of this book.

Not being a dick is one of the most important steps to becoming a great leader.

Dicks are terrible leaders.

I don't think anyone sets out to be a dick. Well-intentioned people just make a couple bad decisions, they take some wrong turns, they listen to the wrong advice and they end up... well, being a dick.

How To Manage A Team Like A Decent And Reasonable Human Being is my attempt to help people who want to be great leaders avoid taking a wrong turn onto Baggadicks Boulevard.

Earlier in my career, I almost made that wrong turn.

I didn't understand what was really important.

Luckily, I had some experiences that showed me the light.

Me and my best friend at work were sitting around and complaining about our manager (who was a dick) and I had an idea. I said we should both find another person and the four of us should get together once a month to talk about stuff.

What kinds of stuff?

My thought was that there were too many dicks managing teams in the company. We were hard-working dynamos who were full of brilliant ideas, but no one would listen to us because of our low levels.

I said we should get a four-person group together to meet once a month and the agenda would be the same every time: how to get ahead in your career after kicking ass at your job.

We were all kicking ass at our jobs, but none of us were getting anywhere. I hypothesized that we needed to get together and talk specifically about how we could get ahead and gain the influence and authority that we would need to help make the company a better place.

We were frustrated, but we were also motivated. When we got together, we talked about office politics, which terrible managers were causing problems, which great managers we wanted to emulate, and why people who were less talented and hard-working than us were getting ahead.

We met for a while. We had the same discussions. Each more frustrating than the last. People just didn't understand our value!

Then something changed.

I got a new boss.

She wasn't a dick.

She empowered and inspired me in a way I'd never been empowered or inspired before. She coached me and developed me. She *talked* to me. She actually seemed to care about me as a person.

Suddenly I didn't care about being woefully under-paid or never getting promoted. Being at level 3 and reporting to someone at level 6 no longer bothered me (even though I knew I should have been like level 5 if we're being realistic).

These things didn't bother me because I was too busy coming up with ideas and implementing them. I was too busy being empowered by an amazing boss.

After a while, I started to talk to my discussion group less and less about all the dicks in the company and more and more about all the things she was doing. We wondered where she learned to manage like that (she didn't go to Harvard or work at NASA or serve in the Oval Office).

My group and I had talked about our favorite leadership books and, though she did a lot of the good things from the books, she didn't seem to be following any sort of model or script.

After a while, I finally arrived at the truth of what made her such an amazing manager.

All she did was act like a decent and reasonable human being.

Could it be so simple?

I studied her for years, watching how she interacted with people, paying attention to her actions and motivations, and I kept coming back to the same conclusion.

The thing that truly set her apart was that she acted like a decent and reasonable human being.

It sounds so simple and, in theory, it is... much like, in theory, putting a rocket on the moon is easy. I mean, you just get some really powerful thrusters and aim for the big white circle.

I assure you that, although she made it look easy,

managing like a decent and reasonable human being is exceedingly difficult.

Why is it so hard?

Because it doesn't benefit *you* in the least.

Managing like a decent and reasonable human being makes life great for everyone who reports to you. Managing like a decent and reasonable human being makes your organization more effective. Managing like a decent and reasonable human being makes the world a better place.

But it doesn't benefit you.

Not necessarily, not directly.

Not unless you're the kind of person who cares.

Not unless you've seen what poor management does and you just have an innate desire to do better.

Some people don't feel this way.

Some people think of their career as a game where the company is a tool to be manipulated for personal gain and the other employees are contestants working against them.

These people think they need to do whatever it takes to get ahead because they view their career as a personal conquest rather than a servant role to make an organization and the people in it better.

If you are one of those people, this book might not be for you (even if you can handle the potty words). If you think of your career as a game with winners and losers - and have no interest in changing - I would encourage you to stop reading, return this book, and get your money back.

If you've found yourself playing games in your career

(like I did) and haven't really seen a better way, but want to change to be a better servant leader, then I invite you to read on and learn all you can.

Life is just a series of learning opportunities and experience is the best teacher. My hope is that my experiences will enrich your journey and speed up your development.

You can make a pretty big difference by managing like a decent and reasonable human being.

PART I

PREPARING YOURSELF

1

THE MOTIVATION TO LEAD

My career goals have changed over the years, but one of those goals has remained constant: to retire.

I've worked for longer than I care to. I think we all have.

Along the way, I've had tons of managers.

Here's what I've learned: most managers suck.

They all don't suck on a technical level. That is to say, they can fill out all the HR forms and assign work and maybe even do some team building events (if they're in the top 20%).

They can show up every day fully bathed and go through the motions of getting a little bit of work done while raging against the incredible undercurrent of the corporate machine.

But they still suck.

I thought about this a lot when I reflected on the sucky managers that I hated.

"Why do I hate them? Why do they suck?" I'd ask myself silently as I stared at them with dumbfounded incredulity from across the cube farm.

What I came to realize is that these managers weren't necessarily bad managers, they were bad people.

Maybe they weren't black-hearted, mustache-twirling villains, but they just weren't nice when they went about their managerial duties.

Succinctly put, they acted like dicks.

I remember one high-profile assignment very clearly. I asked clarifying questions to make sure I knew specifically what my manager wanted. I ran preliminary ideas past them to make sure they were onboard. Then I busted my ass delivering a *great* final product, which I presented to executive leadership.

The second a VP raised an eyebrow, that manager, who was with me agreeing every single step of the way, threw me under a bus.

After the bus ran me over, they waved and jumped up and down to get the bus to stop, then pulled me from behind the bus back to the front tires and told the bus drive to slam on the gas.

I was berated and shouted at in front of my entire team and other leaders.

"What were you doing this whole month... This isn't what we pay you to do... I told you to do this right... "

This example has nothing to do with being a poor project manager or not being able to prioritize work. This isn't, "Oh, I missed that part of manager training when I stepped out for a phone call."

This is just being a dick.

I think way more than half of the managers I've ever had would throw me under the bus to avoid looking even the slightest bit bad in front of someone that outranked them.

"Well of course," you're saying, everyone knows most managers are dicks.

But why?

It's because so many people want to be a manager (hilariously and incorrectly called a "people leader" by some misguided HR teams) for the wrong reasons:

- To get a raise
- To have more power
- To advance their careers
- To show the world how great they are
- So no one can ever tell them what to do again (which, is also hilariously incorrect)

At the same time, these behaviors snuff out a lot of people who could be really great managers. I've heard plenty of promising leaders tell me they don't want to get into management because they don't want to compete against unethical pricks who are chasing the title for the reasons listed above.

It's sad that people don't want to do this for the right reasons.

So what are the right reasons?

Well, if you're going to be entrusted with managing a group of people (not resources, not headcount, but people - people with lives, families, and dreams) you need to be in the right mindset, the servant mindset.

You should want to be a manager to:

- Help your people do more than they could on their own
- Help your people be better employees and better humans
- Help your team be a driver to an organization

Notice the difference between the two lists?

You really can't do them both.

You can't help people do more than they could on their own if you're preoccupied with getting a promotion. You can't help people be better human beings if you're focused on showing the world how great you are. You can't help a team drive positive change in an organization if your primary goal is to get a raise.

You have to focus on the right things.

There's so much emphasis on goal alignment and cross-functional status communications and TPS reports, that managers forget that the most important part of leading a team is just being a decent and reasonable human being.

That's it.

If you do that, you're already in the top 10 percent of all managers.

As sad as it is, it's true. Just ask a random sampling of people in your organization that report to a middle manager and I'll wager most of them agree.

Forget about the latest fad that your Big 4 consultants are trying to sell your executives. It's the same one they're selling your competitors and it's not going to do you any good, anyways. I know that reimagining the framework, bending the curve, torquing the outcomes, or whatever nonsense buzzword catchphrase is in season this month sounds amazing and necessary, but I promise you, it pales in comparison to being a decent and reasonable human being.

That's what this book is about.

The only reason you should bother reading past chapter one of this book is because you don't want to be like all the other terrible managers out there.

If you want to manage the right way, for the right reasons, to have a positive impact on people, on businesses, on the world in general, instead of just checking boxes in unfulfilling monotony for 40 years and making everyone around you feel hopeless and uninspired, then read on and manage like a decent and reasonable human being!

2

THE ATTITUDE TO LEAD

I've worked for a lot of companies and been through some tough stretches. I remember working for a large company during a season of intense transformation.

It was one of the roughest parts of my career, I felt like I was going through the wringer every day.

I know "going through the wringer" is a tired cliché, but it's how I actually felt.

Have you ever seen a wringer?

My great grandma had one. It was a contraption they used before washers and dryers were invented. The wringer was the predecessor to the dryer. It was two rollers, super close together, with a crank (the fancy ones like my great grandma had ran on electricity).

You'd feed your clean wet clothes through it and the wringer would basically crush them, pressing out all the water. I was always told to be careful around it because if I got my hand too close, it would suck my arm in and rip it off.

It certainly looked capable.

That's how I felt when I was working through this transformative season. Every day, I would get up early, immediately log in over breakfast, take calls in my car, work on the bus, get to the office and just bust hump non-stop until I came home, at which time I would have dinner, get the kids to bed, then log back in and work until I was exhausted and pass out before doing it all over again.

It was the hardest I ever worked (or at least top five).

The disappointing thing was that my efforts didn't seem to be having any impact. Executives kept changing direction, work paths hit dead ends, teams weren't communicating so weeks' worth of work had to be re-done all the time.

It felt hopeless.

People burned out; people checked out. A lot of the old timers said stuff like, "Bruce, you're working too hard. None of this matters." Plenty of people just coasted because everything felt so pointless.

I didn't think of it in these terms then, but looking back, I see I was at a crossroads.

I had a decision to make. I could let go and become a floater like so many other people. I could decide to stop trying so hard and wait to see if things changed and got easier. I could just fade into the scenery and not bother.

I didn't, though.

I couldn't.

It's not that I didn't want to. Trust me, I like chilling

out and not being stressed as much as the next guy, but it didn't feel right.

I pushed ahead, I raged against the dying of the light. I put everything I had into trying to improve a seemingly impossible situation.

To this day, I'm still not sure if it mattered, but I do know this: it felt good. As much as it was draining, it felt right. I felt good about myself because of how I handled it.

I later realized that this big decision point was just like every other decision point I'd ever been at. It was just on a larger scale.

Every day I go into work, I have small decision points.

There's days when I think my meeting schedule will keep me from being productive and I have to choose between mailing it in or pressing to do more. There's times when my partners miss a deadline and I have to choose between using it as a free pass to screw around for a couple days or looking for other ways to keep moving forward. There's days when I go into the office just feeling "meh" and knowing that if I just took one day of slacking off and not doing anything, that no one would probably notice.

The decision to fade into the background or do great things comes up every day. It comes in big decision points and tiny decision points. Most people seem to have a spot on that continuum where, when the decision gets too big, the odds of success seem so low, the amount of progress you can make seems so trivial, that they give in and say "That's my limit, I'm not going to try anymore."

It's understandable.

Some would even say it's logical.

But in a management capacity, mailing it in isn't just about your productivity for the day or week or month, it's about an entire team of people.

You can't give in if you want to manage like a decent and reasonable human being.

It's hard to keep a work ethic up in tough times, and it's even harder to do as a manager.

Managing like a decent and reasonable human being is exhausting. It's so much easier to say "Nuts to this!" and just be a dick.

Someone screwed up? Yell at 'em.

Mad at a decision? Stop trying.

Don't like someone? Fire 'em.

It's common.

It's logical.

But it's not reasonable. It's not decent.

It won't help you help your people do more than they could on their own.

It won't help you help your people be better employees and better humans.

It won't help you help your team be a driver to an organization.

It's not easy.

Being a manager isn't easy.

Managing like a decent and reasonable human being is even harder.

If you want to do it, you need to be in the right mindset. You need to accept the difficulty of doing something right for the greater good because you want to benefit others and not just yourself.

Or just forget about it and be a dick.

PART II

THE 11 SIMPLE STEPS

3

MOTIVATE YOUR TEAM

I consider myself to be self-motivated.

You probably consider yourself to be self-motivated, too.

Newsflash: everyone thinks of themselves as self-motivated

No one comes into work thinking, "Boy, I really want to do some work today, but I just can't do anything unless Tony Robbins is there to pump me up."

Sure, motivational speeches and words of encouragement are great (and everyone needs them, even people who say they don't, even you, even me), but that's not all there is to it.

The first ingredient in motivating your team is to not de-motivate them.

You know what's demotivating?

Having a boss that's a dick.

If you've ever gone to the hilarious website despair.-

com, you've seen all their great demotivational posters that say things like "Integrity: play by the rules, get beat by those who don't" and "Micromanagement: a job worth doing is worth doing right over your shoulder by your boss."

These aren't funny because we love liars and micromanagement, they're funny because we use laughter as a coping mechanism. These things are so prevalent that it's sad to the point where you need to laugh so that you don't start screaming and throwing things.

Be a decent and reasonable human being and you'll take yourself out of the running for de-motivating people and you can get on with actually motivating them.

The key to motivation is understanding that people are motivated by different things.

Ask most people what they're motivated by and they'll say money.

But it isn't true.

This is the default answer because most people don't know what they're actually motivated by.

Some people actually have figured out what they're motivated by. Those people usually also just say "money" to avoid feeling awkward or getting mocked by the people who say "money" because they don't actually know what they're motivated by.

Money seems like a logical answer. Very few people would show up to work every day if they weren't getting paid, but that's just a blunt force need, it's not true, transcendental, world-changing motivation.

What if your boss told you that they would give you another $10 if you worked harder?

Would you work harder?

At best, you'd give me some half-assed explanation like it's too small of a percentage to measure and "working harder" is a tough concept to blah blah blah whatever.

What about the last time you got a raise? What about the last time you got a bonus? Those are meaningful amounts of money.

Did you show up to work the next day and say "Wow, I am going to try *so* much harder today"?

Be honest with yourself. You didn't. You may have been a little happier, but you weren't motivated.

Money doesn't truly motivate us.

People accomplish great things all the time without being motivated by money.

My website, HowToRuinYourCompany.com, runs on WordPress. WordPress actually powers over one-third of the ten million most popular websites in the world. It runs over sixty million sites worldwide.

And it's free.

It's open source software.

People write plugins and updates and all sorts of support packs and they don't get paid a damn thing.

Clearly money isn't the motivation there.

Same with Linux. It's open-source software. It's used by virtually every Fortune 500 company and no one made money off of it.

You know where I got those stats?

Wikipedia.

It's the most comprehensive knowledgebase in the history of mankind. You can find anything from a list of honeybee pheromones to the results of the men's Greco-

Roman welterweight competition at the 1960 Olympics to the life story of Velia Abdel-Huda, the first Muslim woman to study at Oxford University (just a few of topics I found from hitting the "Random Article" feature).

You can find pretty much any piece of information anyone has ever known. It was all put there by over a million people (including me) and they all have the same salary.

Zero dollars and zero cents.

The largest collection of information in the world, which is given away for free on a site with no ads, was assembled without anyone getting paid. Jimmy Wales, who started and still owns the site, has never made a dime off of it.

Money is not the primary motivator for most of the world's greatest accomplishments.

Pharaohs didn't build pyramids so they could charge admission (they wanted to be remembered). Alexander the Great didn't conquer the known world to raise taxes (he did it out of revenge).

Heck, the most rewarding job I ever had in my career came at a time when I was managing a bunch of people who ranked below me... and made more than me.

Did it bruise my ego a little? Sure.

Did I think it was unfair? Maybe a little.

But I loved it.

Why?

I had a great boss who was supportive and empowering. I was managing a great team of fun people who worked hard. I was directly connected to meaningful work.

It was awesome. With all that great stuff, I wasn't going home and grumbling about people who made more than me.

But a funny thing happened.

A reorg came through. I lost my team; I got a new boss.

Suddenly, I wasn't feeling supported or empowered. I was kept in the dark on a lot of information and planning. I no longer felt connected to meaningful work.

That was when I started grumbling crap like "I don't get paid enough for this."

It wasn't until I grumbled that crap to the right person that they taught me something I hadn't realized about myself, about people in general:

People only complain about their salary when they aren't happy about their job.

I was making a salary I knew was below market. I was leading people who were a level below me who made more than me.

And I loved it.

I was making the exact same amount a year later and actually had a job that required less work... and that was when I started complaining about money.

Money was not a motivating factor for me.

It's not a motivating factor for the people who contribute to Wikipedia or WordPress, either. It's not a motivating factor for people who go on mission trips to install wells in third world countries.

If you want to manage like a decent and reasonable human being, you need to get past the myth that money is a motivator and that your job as a leader isn't motivation.

People want to feel like they are a part of something.

People want a challenge. People want to feel like they've accomplished something and contributed to a greater good. People want to feel like they've shared their expertise to make the world a better place.

Give it to them.

4

FLOAT ABOVE GOSSIP

One time, I was at lunch in the company cafeteria. Usually, I have meetings over lunch, but on this particular day, I was working on a presentation and really needed to focus alone.

The cafeteria was pretty packed, so it was hard to find a quiet space. I found a two-person table near the wall right next to a small table where two women were already done eating. I figured this would be as good a place as any since they were done and would be leaving soon... or so I thought.

I set up my laptop and started looking over my presentation as I ate my lunch, which did not have too much sodium and definitely didn't have multiple desserts. As I tried to enjoy my very healthy meal and focus on my presentation, I kept getting distracted by the conversation next to me.

One woman was very upset about "the lazy kids" on her floor. Apparently, a software development team had moved onto her floor and she was appalled at their work habits.

"Most of them don't even get in until *nine o'clock!*" she said, making sure everyone in the cafeteria knew how incredulous she found that fact. This woman made it very clear that she came in every day by *eight* o'clock. She also stayed until exactly five o'clock every day and "these kids" all seemed to leave at different times.

I kept eating my nutritious meal, but I could not for the life of me focus on my presentation, I was too fascinated by the conversation going on next to me! I kept staring at my laptop so it wouldn't look like I was eavesdropping while I was eavesdropping, but I wasn't thinking about my presentation at all. I was only thinking about this woman and her story and how emphatic she was.

She talked about their sloppy shirts, their piercings, the way they laughed when they were working. Basically, she talked about everything they did (except if they actually got any work done), and she was angry about all of it.

I finished my entire lunch, which took a while (not because I had double servings of tacos with more beans and rice than I needed and three different desserts because I couldn't make up my mind, though) and she was still ranting.

There were a few things I became aware of.

One was that none of the things this woman was so upset over really mattered. This meant that all of her energy was wasted on things that didn't matter. The second thing I became aware of was that this presentation was not getting done and I was going to blame ADHD. The third thing was that this woman's friend hadn't really said a thing except for a few times when she tried (unsuccessfully) to politely end the conversation and get back to work.

Nothing doing, though, because Angry Ranter just steamrolled her with more (mostly repeated) complaints about appearance, hours, and ping pong - can you believe they actually played ping pong at the ping pong table!?

So this woman was upset about things that didn't matter (like repeatedly insisting for some reason that eight o'clock to five o'clock was the only time work could get done), took an incredible amount of time complaining about it (she was done eating when I arrived and still ranting when I left an hour later), wasted a ton of her friend's time (while making her visibly uncomfortable for the duration of the conversation), and (worst of all) distracted me from my probably very important presentation.

All because it feels good to complain.

Which it does.

There's a bonding element that comes into play when we gossip. There's also a personal validation that comes from complaining to someone about someone else - it makes us feel like someone else "gets it" and agrees with us, so we must be right (even if the other person is clearly uncomfortable and trying to remove themselves from the situation)

But there's nothing healthy about this. There's nothing productive about this. There's nothing decent and reasonable about this.

If you have a problem with someone, you should talk to them about it, not bitch to someone else about it.

You don't need to be all full of fire and vitriol, either, you just have a calm conversation like a decent and reasonable human being where you explain your perspective and listen to try to understand theirs.

"Excuse me, but I was just curious about your team. Do you guys have a set schedule? How do you manage your work and deadlines? I know your work is different than my work, and your team is different than my team, so I'm just trying to understand different work styles. Would you mind talking about it a little?"

You'll be happier. They'll be happier. The world will be a better place.

Gossiping is like eating a double taco lunch with three desserts: it may feel good in the moment, but it's a bad idea long term (or so I've heard).

Gossip does you no good as a person and it can tear a team apart if you do it as a manager.

I had a manager gossip about me once.

Back in college, I had a few jobs writing code. I was also taking programming courses in school. I was at one of these jobs when a friend had a scripting question. It was similar to something I had done in one of my classes.

Since all my work was available online, I just pulled up the page I'd put together. The page had all kinds of code on it: search algorithms, scripts, even a video of a dragon (because dragons are badass).

I sorted through it all, found the code my friend needed and went about my day of writing awesome code and doing great things.

Little did I know that my boss was walking behind me when I pulled up my page. He saw me looking at a screen that had all my assignments, including, among other things, a video of a badass dragon.

My boss didn't say anything, though.

At least not to me.

But a few days later, he complained to a co-worker that I was just sitting around looking at dinosaur videos all day.

Not only did he not come to me with his concern, not only did he gossip about it to someone else, but (maybe the most unforgivable part) he thought my badass dragon was a dinosaur!

A freaking dinosaur!

That last part may only be important to me, but the lesson to learn about managing like a decent and reasonable human being is to not gossip, to just go directly to people and talk to them.

This seems like a silly little misunderstanding on the surface, but it really bothered me and forever tempered my opinion of this man.

He walked around for days thinking I was some kind of slacker. I'm sure that had an impact on his subconscious perception of me even after it was cleared up. He also showed that he took a distanced approach to leadership. On top of it all, it just made me feel bad that he would complain about me behind my back (especially when there was nothing to complain about)

This is not how decent and reasonable human beings act.

It's definitely not how decent and reasonable human beings manage.

If he saw my badass dragon video and just leaned over

my shoulder and said "Hey, why are you looking at dinosaur videos?" I could have let him know it was a dragon and then explained that it was a page that had some sample code that we needed to look at for our very important work.

And the whole episode would have been avoided.

He wouldn't have had to wonder about my work ethic. He wouldn't have had to complain to my co-worker about it. My co-worker wouldn't have had to hear unfounded criticisms and been put in the difficult situation of having to be the person to tell me about it. And I wouldn't have had to be upset with him.

It can be hard to confront someone directly, but it can be done tactfully, with kindness and respect, and it can avoid a lot of problems down the line.

It can feel awkward, but, like I said, managing like a decent and reasonable human being isn't easy.

5

ENGAGE YOUR PEOPLE

E ngagement is one of the most misunderstood concepts in leadership.

It's like some mythical beast that no one truly understands and a lot of people talk about engagement in the wrong context.

Sure, high engagement scores look good on your review and engagement drives productivity through the roof, but the real reason managers should aim for engagement is this:

It's just the decent and reasonable thing to do.

You do things like daily standups and work boards to increase productivity (as long as you do them right), but the biggest benefit to increasing engagement isn't productivity (though that can come): it's just making the workplace better, enriching the people on your team.

Don't seek out high engagement scores. That number should be a representation of everything that's being done, it should not be a goal in and of itself. So many companies misuse this metric and it leads to toxic behaviors and even lower engagement than they had in the first place.

Companies botch their engagement plans all the time and "help" managers who score low with fun "coaching" (that is decidedly not fun) from HR and higher-ups.

When managers have engagement quotas looming over their heads with all sorts of other priorities, this kind of additional pressure drives things in the wrong direction.

I've worked with managers who threaten their teams if scores don't go up.

Now, they don't come in pimp-strutting and lean over and whisper "if that 'I have the tools necessary to do my job' score doesn't come in higher than a 4, you're getting a shank in the copier room at lunch time," but they do say things like "if our scores don't go up, they're gonna make it hard on me, hard on all of us - I know things aren't perfect, but low scores will just make it worse."

"But Bruce," I can hear some of you asking, "how can I get my team to be more engaged without veiled threats?"

Easy - by being engaging!

I'm not talking about a forced smile and well-rehearsed small talk with realistic-sounding laughter, I'm talking about being a decent and reasonable human being!

Talk to your team (some people might even call this "engaging" with your team).

In another book of mine (shameless self-promotion alert), Leave Work Early And Go To The Bar, I talk about all the benefits of talking to the people on your team and getting to know them. For now, I'll focus on one small piece of it: if you have a good relationship with your team, they will talk to you more.

Now, I'm not saying to force a relationship and pretend to care so you can dupe them into raising their engagement scores, I'm talking about getting to know them so you will understand what they want.

You could simply talk to your team ahead of time to see which areas of engagement they might think are lacking and see what suggestions they might have for improving things. Then you could, you know, improve things.

One of the approaches I've used was handing out a paper version of the engagement survey in a team meeting and asking everyone to submit their scores anonymously. That way, I already knew what was keeping them from deeper engagement and I could try to do something about it.

I didn't do this because I wanted HR to see I could get high scores (after all, I could achieve that with less effort just by threatening them). I did it to make our workplace better, to make our team better, to make the company a better place. I did this to manage like a decent and reasonable human being.

You might be starting from a low point, but this approach can still work wonders. Odds are near certain that your team will be so thrilled just knowing that you even care, that their engagement will increase just as a result of having the discussion.

Having open discussions about the things that may be bothering your team and then doing something about those things is a decent and reasonable thing to do. I mean, doesn't it just *sound* reasonable?

This type of open dialogue doesn't fix things overnight, but it sets you down a long journey of deeper understanding that leads to true connection and engagement. The more you ask your team and take their perspectives into account, the more comfortable they will be sharing heavier things, revealing your own blind spots, coming up with ideas you hadn't thought of, and making everything about your team better.

These discussions are the heart of engagement for people who manage like decent and reasonable human beings.

Yes, you can coerce people into higher engagement *scores*, but you can't actually improve *engagement* by any disingenuous means.

You can't increase engagement by putting up a ping pong table and then giving everyone the stink eye when they go to play ping pong and grumble about how "nothing ever gets done when you're all over there playing ping pong."

People see right through this nonsense. It wastes everyone's time and generally pisses them off. You will decrease engagement and motivation, and everyone will basically hate you (and they'll probably gossip about you because that's the kind of environment you're fostering).

Instead, be a decent and reasonable human being. Talk openly with your people. Don't judge them. Welcome feedback. You'd be surprised at how engaging this can be.

6

DON'T BOTHER MICROMANAGING

Working closely with your people is a decent and reasonable thing to do, but it's possible to go too far.

There's a lot of stories about overbearing managers who don't trust their people and become micromanagers.

What you don't hear about as much are well-intentioned managers who want to help their people but end up unintentionally micromanaging instead.

It can be a tough balance, even when we have the best intentions.

Too often, we give someone an assignment with a laundry list of requirements. Make sure the first slide starts with the problem statement. Make sure you have a sans serif font. Make sure the taco bar doesn't use canned salsa.

We do this because we want to make sure everything is "perfect," but we end up being textbook micromanagers (but seriously, the taco bar should never use canned salsa).

I've had a number of great managers in my career, but one really sticks out on how she avoided micromanaging.

When she gave me an assignment, she would monitor how I was doing and wait to give me coaching until I needed it. This was a great tactic to avoid micromanaging.

Her feedback was great, too. She didn't just say "make sure the taco bar doesn't use canned salsa," instead she would say "the last time we did a taco bar, everyone loved it but the canned salsa got a lot of complaints."

This comes across as a helpful insight rather than a demanding order. It's a small thing, the kind of thing we dismiss when we're in a hurry, but it really helps.

My manager always took the time to phrase her feedback along the lines of "If you do it that way, do you think the CFO might feel like you're not hearing him?" or "I really like this, but do you think it ties back to the strategy map close enough for people to make the connection?"

She always used her wisdom and experience to guide me and enlighten me, she never once said "shut up and do it my way." She may have said "I understand where you're coming from, but I would really like you to do it this way" once every year or so, and after twelve months of handling things great, it didn't really bother me.

When I had important slides and reports, we'd look them over together and she never micromanaged. She could have picked at every detail and made tiny little changes all over. She could have switched my adjective and made my borders a different color and used more underlining instead of italicizing, but she didn't.

The details she could have meddled with were also so trivial that they didn't really change the point of any of the documents. Now, if there was a major gaffe, something misleading or confusing, or an obviously universally atrocious design element (like a dinosaur), I would have expected her to point it out. But since things were reasonably decent, she left them all alone.

She realized that pretty much every one of those minor changes around font and color would have been a personal preference. She may have liked it better, but it was a 50-50 proposition that the audience would have liked it better and if the audience had more than 3 people, it was probably a wash, anyways.

She also realized that a bunch of ticky-tacky updates like that would have been a time suck with an end result of just ticking me off. So she let them go. She empowered me. She macro-managed me.

She focused on the results more than the details.

If the documents I was putting together were getting the point across in a clear and professional manner, the little details didn't matter.

Remember that.

In almost everything in the business world, the bulk of the little details don't matter.

It's not to say they aren't important or you shouldn't be detailed-oriented, but your preferred way of aligning text compared to someone else on the team's preferred way of aligning text doesn't really make a lick of difference at the end of the day (as long as we all agree that it's explicitly incorrect to put two spaces after a period).

When my amazing boss let those things go, when she

let me do my work in my own style, it was invigorating. It pushed me to work at a higher level of quality because I knew I owned it. Whatever I did wasn't just going to get run over and completely re-worked, it would be used. My work mattered.

In addition to that, it made me acutely aware of when I was encroaching on doing any of those micro-manager behaviors to my own team. This in turn, made me manage them differently, I let them do their work in their own style, which invigorated them and let them know their work mattered.

This also made me a more productive manager in addition to a more popular one. If I wasn't spending time changing fonts and verb choices (which is hard for me to resist as a writer), it freed up a lot of time to do things that would actually matter (although I absolutely used find and replace to get rid of any points where anyone tried to sneak two spaces in after a period).

7

EMPOWER YOUR PEOPLE

Once a manger is reasonable enough to get out of the micro-managing game, they can get to the next level: the empowerment level - this is where you really help your people rock out!

You want your people to grow into dynamos, right?

Well, you have to give your people responsibility if you want them to grow.

Some managers seem to feel scared that their people will grow.

It's like they have some subconscious insecurity that their people will outperform them and make them look bad, so they try to keep them down. They don't outright oppress them. They still help them look good, but they make sure not to let them look too good. Not better than them, anyway.

That's not decent and reasonable, that's just acting like a dick.

There are way too many reasons why managers don't

empower their people more, but one of the biggest reasons is that managers think they know best. There's no shame in that (we all think we're pretty smart), but we need to get over it.

If we can't get past that, we put ourselves in situations where we really want to empower people, but we think *this* project is too important. We have thoughts like "Well, things are really tough right now, so I can't trust Ricky Bobby with this project. I'll take the lead on getting through this really hard part (so I don't burden poor Ricky Bobby) and then maybe he can take on the next project."

Get over it.

You're working with adults (or at least children of working age), so treat them like it.

Give them those tough opportunities. I understand the logic behind why managers don't want to, but when you put training wheels on your people, you're stunting their growth. Just hold on to the back of the seat and run alongside them - they'll learn a lot quicker.

Decent and reasonable human beings give their people a chance to own projects and learn and (hopefully) succeed (don't worry, we'll talk about handling failure, later).

We get trapped in these circles of unintentional disempowerment in the name of "protecting" our people.

We need to break those cycles.

We need to empower our people if we want to help them do more than they could on their own.

Another reason that managers end up not empowering their people is just plain laziness.

There's a big misconception out there about what

empowerment actually is. As much as it sounds great to just throw work at people and say "deal with it, suckas," that isn't empowerment, that's absentee management.

Empowerment takes time.

Empowerment is about giving your people responsibilities instead of just assignments. But when you empower people, you still have a large stake in helping them be successful.

It would be foolish to turn over a large, critical project to someone you barely know and then hope it all works out.

You would set them up for failure and make yourself look bad in the process. Optics and politics aside, it's just not a decent or reasonable thing to do.

To get value from empowerment, you need to be training, supporting, and championing your people. You need to work directly with them to make sure they're doing everything right (without micromanaging). You need to share the full breadth and depth of your wisdom and experience to ensure they're making decisions with as much knowledge as possible (knowledge is power, sharing knowledge is sharing power, sharing power is the definition of empowerment). You need to check up on them and make sure things are progressing in the right direction and provide whatever help they may need when they need it.

Empowerment is exhausting.

Empowerment isn't just trusting and coaching and helping, though - it also means taking a backseat in the decisions.

If you've empowered someone with something, I mean

truly empowered them, that means they have the final say in it.

If you get to a decision point and you think the rollout should be put on hold, but the person you empowered to lead the effort thinks it should move forward, what do you do?

Empowerment means giving someone power. That means the power to make decisions.

Amazon uses a great management principle called Disagree and Commit. It's pretty self-explanatory. It means you don't have to agree with every decision in order to support it and help it be successful.

Sure, when it comes to your boss, you disagree and you commit all the time, but that's because they're above you on the org chart and you like getting paychecks and buying things like food. You might grumble under your breath, but you support the things that your boss tells you to do even when you don't think it's the best path.

If you truly want to empower someone, you need to disagree and commit with someone *below* you on the org chart.

You probably have reasons why you think the launch should be put on hold. If you're doing your job as an empowering manager, you should have been giving your teammate all your perspective and thoughts you've had along the way.

You should be helping them understand all the things that could happen, help them understand the impacts of various scenarios, and tell them the relatable stories of successes and failures you've had in the past that can help them navigate this decision.

Then let them make the decision.

And help it be successful.

Even if you disagree.

It's hard to try to make a direction successful if we don't think it's a good idea, but by golly, you do it when your boss tells you to do it, so flex those same muscles to help your teammate be successful.

No cheating, either. Be genuine.

You can't say things like "Well, it's your decision, but you'd be stupid to move forward with this rollout."

That's passive-aggressively manipulating someone into doing things your way. That's not decent and reasonable. That's not empowerment.

As Obi Wan once told Luke "Let go."

You have to let go of power if you want to empower someone.

Once you make it over that mental hurdle, you aren't out of the woods yet. More challenges await that need to be handled in a decent and reasonable manner.

If their move proves successful, you have to give them credit.

As the manager of the area, people will undoubtedly talk to you about it and tell you that was a good move.

This is your cue to give your teammate the credit.

However, this is where so many managers choose, subconsciously to be a dick instead of a decent and reasonable human being.

They don't give Susie Mae all her well-deserved credit for making a courageous decision that her boss didn't agree with and being proved right. Instead, they think something along the lines of "Well, I'm in charge of the team and I made the decision to let her choose the path, so yes, I deserve some credit here" then they nod at the person who complimented them and say, with a forced smile of false humility, "It's all in a day's work."

Here's the thing: it's very hard for us to receive a compliment and think "I don't really deserve this." We're wired to enjoy getting compliments. That type of positive reinforcement plays into human psychology in a way that drives us to want to do great things. This is why it feels so unnatural for us to turn down a compliment and give the credit to someone else.

It's hard, but it's not complicated. Just say something like "Well, I had Susie Mae running point and she did great." You can even throw in a "I think she's really going places."

If you push yourself and try hard, you can react this way. If you practice it enough it will - like anything else - become easier.

Eventually, it becomes invigorating.

It becomes liberating, too. It reminds you and reinforces the fact (to you and everyone else) that nothing on a team gets done all by one person.

But what if Susie Mae ends up being wrong?

What if that decision that you supported - even though you disagreed with it - ends up being a disaster?

Do you tell her, "I told you so"?

No, that would be a dick move.

So instead you say "Look, Susie Mae, I understand why you made the decisions you did. It took courage to stand up and set that direction. But looking back, now you can see why I was right."

That's just being a dick while pretending to not be a dick. A rose by any other name...

You have to coach Susie Mae through this in a positive manner. Ask her what she learned (without being condescending). Think through what you've learned. Share your thoughts openly with her so she can learn from them (leaving out all the thoughts you are having about how right you are and how all of this could have been avoided if she'd done things your way). You can learn just as much as she can from her screw ups.

And just like people will want to talk to you when things go well, people will also want to talk to you if they don't go well.

Oh yes, those are entirely different conversations and it seems like a lot more people come out of the woodwork for those.

This is a test for you as a manager. This is where the true test of empowerment comes.

This is where you need to be Susie Mae's shit shield.

You can't just say "Yeah, what a disaster. This is what happens when I let Susie Mae make the call. Don't worry, I won't make that mistake again."

That's not fair. You let her make the decision and you have some accountability there.

But wait, you didn't get to take credit for Susie Mae's good work, so why do you have to take blame for her screw up - isn't that a double standard?

Yup.

Deal with it.

That's the accountability you took on when you assumed management of an entire team. That's what you signed up for when you read past chapter one and bound yourself by a blood oath to manage like a decent and reasonable human being.

There's a train of thought that says Susie Mae needs to face the music, that she won't "learn her lesson" unless she takes the brunt of it.

Don't worry, Susie Mae knows she screwed up.

You ever screwed up?

How did it feel?

Did it feel great until someone pointed it out? Or did you know right away that you messed up, even if people didn't line up to point it out to you?

Rubbing her nose in it or pushing her to the front of the blame queue doesn't help her learn and grow and gain confidence for future decisions. That's not empowerment and it's not tough love. If you don't help mitigate some of the negative impact (or worse yet, if you fuel it with comments like "I told her not to do it") then you aren't empowering her, you're hanging her out to dry.

Half-hearted attempts at being decent and reasonable don't count, either. You can't say, "yeah, it's a team effort, we all have our part. I mean, Susie Mae had the final decisions, but you know..." You need to genuinely help.

To manage like a decent and reasonable human being, you need to absorb some blame when it hits and share the credit when it comes.

8

BE A CHAMPION

Giving Susie Mae credit for her correct decision that you disagreed with is a big part of empowerment. It's also one of the first steps in being a champion for your people.

Being a champion means more than just helping your people be successful, it means letting others know about it, too. Your position gives you access to people that your teammates don't have access to. Let those people know how great your teammates actually are.

Now, when Susie Mae needs to give a presentation to Karen from accounting to get her to buy into the next big project, the odds of success are going to go up because this isn't the first time Karen from accounting ever heard of Susie Mae - she's already heard about how great she is. And if Karen from accounting already thinks Susie Mae is great, she's a lot more likely to react favorably to the presentation.

That's good for Susie Mae, it's good for you, it's good

for the company, it's good for everyone. Letting other people know how great someone is is a decent and reasonable thing to do.

And if someone on your team is really great, championing them goes beyond telling people about it. It goes into making an even more meaningful difference and nominating them for a promotion.

This can get tricky. The number of people that want to be promoted is always greater than the number of people that we want to promote and that number is, in turn, always greater than the number of people HR wants to promote.

I'm going to focus on the last part of that equation right now because that's where we really learn about how hard it can be to champion people.

Most big companies have HR departments that handle promotions like car insurance. They put together a huge list of conditions that have to be met in order to get what you want, but even if you meet every single condition, they still have enough vague disclaimers around it to give them a reason to say no.

That's why you have to be the champion.

I faced an uphill battle like this once. I was managing a team of people who collectively were knocking it out of the park. Most of them hit what the company called "the high bar for success" (which is a fancy way of saying even if you're doing really good, it doesn't mean your review is going to be above average), but there were two in particular that were out-performing the norm for their level by such a wide margin that I had to take action.

They were probably outperforming more than half of

the people in the company who were already at the next level. I really needed to promote them to the next level.

There was only one problem.

On my team, their job family didn't have a next level.

I talked it over with my boss, who agreed that these two superstars were more than deserving of a promotion, but also realized that battling HR was an uphill battle.

Still, I went to HR. I explained that I had amazing people who were outperforming most of the people that were already a level higher and that these two needed a promotion. My HR partners listened to everything I said, nodded in agreement with all my points, and told me they understood how challenging that could feel for me as a manager... then they politely told me to get bent.

I went back to my manager, who of course explained they knew that was going to happen.

I stewed over it for a week, then reached out to HR again and asked *how* exactly new job levels were created. I asked for examples of when it had happened in the past and reached out to those managers to get tips. I went out to lunch with a bunch of people from HR to pick their brains and spitball ideas. Then, when I fully understood everything, all the ins and outs, all the keywords and requirements, I submitted a bulletproof proposal for a new job level that HR just *had to* approve.

And they promptly rejected it.

So I followed up with them yet again. They seemed to be a little miffed, but they didn't realize this was just the beginning of my *fourteen-month* journey to wear them down and finally get the job level approved.

For one of the two people on my team.

It took a couple more months to get it approved for the second person, but I did it.

It was no fun, but I had to do it. Not so I could write a book and brag about persistence (though I admit the story came in handy and I am a little proud of myself), not so my teammates would like me (one of them was never really a fan of me, anyways), not for anything that would benefit me, and not because I wanted them to stay on my team (it was disbanded in a reorg within a year), but simply because it's the decent and reasonable thing to do.

They deserved it and it was the right thing.

The stars on my team got what they deserved, which is really my biggest goal in managing like a decent and reasonable human being.

9

FORGET ABOUT BUILDING EMPIRES

Remember way back at the beginning of this book when we talked about the wrong reasons to want to be a manager? If you don't, I'll save you some page turning and remind you that "power" is one of the general themes.

Power is a self-serving, ego-stroking reason to want to be a manager. There's nothing decent or reasonable about chasing a title for more power.

Nobody thinks that they're chasing power, instead they think things like "Well, I know the best way to move the company forward and other people don't get it, so I need to get to a position of authority so that I can make everyone do things the right way."

I can relate to this mindset. As someone who often thinks their ideas are awesome, I get why people could feel like they need to be in a role of authority to make everyone do things the right way (i.e., *their* way).

But it's not how decent and reasonable human beings manage things.

If you know better than everyone else, your goal shouldn't be to get a promotion - your goal should be to help other people understand things better.

This book is not about how you can help people understand things better (if you need help with that, try Influencer by Grenny and Patterson, Influence Without Authority by Cohen and Bradford, or even the more old-school Machiavellian handbook The Prince by Machiavelli), it's about managing like a decent and reasonable human being.

This chapter is focused on what not to do: specifically, the self-serving activities of building an empire and protecting your turf.

Building an empire is artificially bloating your team size so that you can have a bigger footprint and more weight to throw around.

Managers who build empires like to say things in budget meetings like "well, you have to do the stupid things that I insist on because my team is so gigantic."

They don't actually use those words, but that's the gist of them. If one of these clowns ever manages to get a foothold of power, they will do everything they can to expand it... with no real purpose or benefit.

I saw this firsthand when a new VP came into an organization and got a sizable team. Their immediate message to their peers was "If you want me to do what I came here to do, you need to give me more people!"

This leader couldn't be bothered with goals or targets or outcomes, they kept twisting every conversation back to some version of "but don't you know how important it is?"

Yes (eye roll), we do, it's all important, but good leaders, decent and reasonable human beings, get as much done as they can with their resources (which is usually more than people expect) instead of using it as a sad excuse to grab power.

This "leader" ended up with an $8M budget (it was a lot more than that, but this makes the math easier). In the first quarter, the team spent basically nothing, same in the second quarter. When asked, they insisted they needed it all.

One bright, insightful genius raised a red flag to the executive committee. He said to be careful because this leader could burn all of the budget hiring people at the end of the year, then demand a much higher budget the following year because the team was so big and needed to be sustained.

Everyone scoffed, claiming that would never happen

In the third quarter, hiring picked up to the tune of $2M and in the 4th quarter, the team exploded with hiring and burned through $6M of their $8M.

So his team spent $8M in the year when their budget was $8M. Looks good, right?

Well you're not going to believe what happened next (although the brilliant young analyst I mentioned in the story saw this coming). This leader said that, since his team was spending $6M per quarter, he was going to need $24M next year. That's right, he wanted to triple his budget.

His reasoning?

That's the size staff he needs to do his job.

This, dear reader, is how one builds an empire.

It's not decent and it's not reasonable.

It doesn't help people achieve greatness; it doesn't help organizations serve their customers. It's just a massive ego stroke.

The worst part is, that once an empire is built, it needs to be protected.

I never felt this so acutely as I did with one specific assignment I had where I took over the *entire job* of one of our Big 4 consultants (whose hourly billing rate was roughly my day's wage).

My job was to send an email to a group of executives every month, asking them to send me a status update. Their updates could be no longer than two bullet points, since this need to be concise. Once I received the updates, I was to cut and paste them all into a single document.

Then, I had to email that document to a vice president, who would put it into a central file location and then let the executive vice president know it was ready.

This took roughly 7 to 8 minutes out of my busy schedule each month (which explains why our consultant had so much time to look at his phone and take naps).

Even though it wasn't a lot of time, I still felt compelled to suggest a potentially more efficient way of doing things.

What if, I proposed, we just put the document into the central file location and let all the vice presidents make their own updates? If we put a notification on their calendars, they could make the updates and the executive vice president could just open the document when she needed to. It would be seamless, I said.

An entire high-priced consultant's whole job entirely replaced by a calendar notice. I could win a productivity award for that!

Boy was I naive.

It was "too much work" for the vice presidents to have to make their updates to a central file instead of just emailing them to me, it was "too confusing" for them to have to do the work when a calendar notice reminded them instead of me sending an email reminder, and the whole process would be "too disruptive" to change... or so I was told.

I forgot that this process kept one vice president squarely on the executive vice president's radar every single month.

They would have probably slit my throat to keep that process in place and maintain their position beside a highly influential leader.

Anyone who's worked at a large established company before knows how this stuff works. High-ranking people get really funny about their territory and position. They do everything they can to put up barriers around their access to high-ranking people.

If you make something more efficient, you threaten their access.

Do it anyway.

Decent and reasonable human beings don't make things difficult on everyone just to hold political leverage. Geez, do you even want that? Do you want to be the cause of intentional dysfunction simply to feel powerful?

I don't.

Grow up and do it right.

Instead of spending all that time trying to put together an empire and patrolling the borders to make sure no one is encroaching on their turf, what if - just hear me out - they actually did something productive?

10

BALANCE STRESS AND ACCOUNTABILITY

This book could have been released a lot sooner. It's not that I don't enjoy writing, it's just that there's so many other things I could be doing. I have a day job, a bunch of kids to raise, Netflix to watch, tacos to eat, naps to take - it can get really hard to motivate myself to get a project like this finished.

There was no reason this book *had to* get written. Sure, I was hoping it would help people be better managers and make the world a better place, but couldn't that wait a couple days, especially when I really wanted to take all those naps?

This book wasn't done sooner because I didn't have a deadline. Sure, I could make my own deadline, but if it came and went? Shrug. No biggie. Nothing happens.

We face these same challenges when we're at work. Usually, our people find ways to self-motivate, but as a manager, you still have to play a role.

A little stress can cause action.

One time, I was working at a big company and we were facing unprecedented budget projections early in the year. Finances are always tight, but this year, the demands were really out of control. My vice president asked me what I thought we should do.

Now, I had a lot of experience with garbage nonsense projections. I'm intimately familiar with the games leaders play with their budgets. Usually, they ask for double what they think they'll actually need (even though I know that what they think they actually need is wrong, too, because it's an impossible question to answer correctly).

"I don't know," I said since we were so early in the year that none of this felt like it mattered, "whatever, just give 'em half."

"Well," she said, "the CEO is prepared to release funds, the executive committee is waiting for our team's recommendation, I'm leaving you in charge of the recommendation."

"Ok," I said, "can we talk about-"

"I'm going on vacation," she said. "I need you to put together the recommendation."

Now I had a little stress. Now motivation was coming into play.

This took me from "Well, whatever, these budgets are all imaginary numbers and it'll work out in the end" to "Holy balls, the fate of an iconic institution is resting solely on my shoulders."

Needless to say, I ended up working over the weekend.

I pored through every projection, I analyzed every cost bucket, I compared projected software license charges, pulled up historical records showing what managers projected compared to what they spent in previous years, dove into non-labor contract deals, talked to every straight-talking friend I had inside every project team, and basically looked through every piece of information I could find until I arrived at my conclusion.

No increases for anyone.

That's what the numbers told me.

I didn't believe them at first, so I double checked, slept on it, then checked again. I slept on it again before thinking it over some more and reviewing it again.

That was still my final answer.

The VP who said she was going on vacation actually called me from her vacation. I knew she would do this since, even though she really needed that vacation, she was still a decent and reasonable human being. She empowers her people without being an absentee manager and she knows how to give her people just the right amount of stress to motivate them. When she called, she asked what my recommendation was.

She was a little taken aback by my answer. Understandably so.

I walked her through my process and she asked me if I was sure a few dozen times then reminded me how important it was to not be wrong like seven or eight times. After sticking to my answer through all that she said "Ok, I will support you, but this is on you as much as it's on me."

We took the recommendation to the executive committee and my VP backed me up despite the incredulous reactions (remember when I told you managing like a decent and reasonable human being also entailed being a champion for your people?).

As the year wore on and things played out (mostly) how I expected, we actually finished *under* budget without giving anyone any increases.

Everything worked out amazing.

This isn't a story about how great I was at predicting budget trends in a difficult time (but, you know, ahem) or about how a great leader can champion their people, it was about how a little bit of stress pushed me to work at another level.

I could have mailed it in early and just stuck with "give 'em half." So many people do. I almost did. Most things get done like this because people don't take the effort. They don't need to because we carefully word our goals so that we can meet them no matter what happens.

If everyone just goes through the motions and turns the cranks, a big established multi-billion company probably won't crumble.

But, if you push a little, if you apply just enough stress to motivate (and not enough stress to damage someone's health) at just the right time (not all the time), you can help people achieve more than they could have otherwise - you can help your organization be greater than it otherwise would have.

Some managers think that since a little stress can be a good thing that a lot of stress must be a great thing, so they go out of their way to pile things on.

This is a great way to burn people out and make them hate you. It's not a decent and reasonable way to go about things.

At the same time, with zero stress, there's probably zero drive. Stress is what drives us to do almost everything we do. Human beings are procrastinators by nature - we don't eat until we're hungry and we don't work on projects until it feels like we need to.

Stress can be used as a strategic tool, but it should be something we dig out of the middle of the toolbox when we need it, not the tool that we leave on the counter because we use it nine times a day.

Finding balance is key.

11

LEARN FROM FAILURE

I f you're going to manage a team, you will inevitably have someone who fails.

I don't care how great they are, I don't care how competent they are, at some point, one of them is going to fail.

It's not easy to handle failure like a decent and reasonable human being.

Lots of managers lash out when someone on their team messes up. I'm not sure exactly why. Maybe they think it will teach their people a lesson and make them work harder next time. Maybe they think that's how they're supposed to handle it because they had a manager that treated them that way. Maybe their parents didn't give them enough hugs.

Whatever the reason, it's not a decent and reasonable way to manage.

Lots of managers talk about how they want their people to try new things, but once one of those new things doesn't work out, they go ballistic. They'll say all the catchy buzzword things like "fail fast" and "permission to fail" and "every failure is just another step on the path to success."

Then someone fails and everyone realizes how short the boss expects that path to success to be.

If your top performer messes up a TPS report one day, what will you say? Are you going to get all red-faced and forehead-veined and shout at them, "What are you, stupid? You can't even fill out a TPS report? You'll never make VP like that!"

This isn't decent and reasonable. This isn't helpful. People don't react well to that.

Maybe you'll make the point that they need to not mess up their TPS reports, but the real point that you'll make is that you're a dick.

If you have good people on your team, they'll know when they mess up. They'll feel bad even if you don't yell at them so loud that your forehead vein pops out.

If you yell like that, that person is never going to feel comfortable trying anything new or trying to go above and beyond while they're working for you. They will work in fear of making a mistake instead of feeling empowered and inspired to accomplish great things.

Plus, everyone else is gonna hear about it and make their own judgements, too. No one is going to try extra hard for a manager that unloads on their co-workers like that - especially when they know that they could be the next one to get the forehead-vein treatment.

You can't demean your people.

You can't let their co-workers do it, either.

If Jimmy Ray messes up his TPS report and you are kind, helpful, understanding, gracious, decent, and reasonable when you correct him, but then Bobby James comes in with a smirk and whispers in your ear "Can you believe this guy? He can't even get a TPS report right, he's not getting a bigger bonus than me, is he?" you need to shut that down.

Shut.

It.

Down.

This is toxic.

Don't talk about people on your team like that and don't let anyone else talk about people on your team like that.

It's not about breeding internal resentment and killing morale and productivity, it's just plain not decent and reasonable.

Mistakes are a part of the learning process. I know that sounds like corny sunshine blowing, but it's the truth.

Failure is a part of the learning process - nobody learns without failing.

Humans are actually built to learn through failing. We see this from the earliest stages of human development.

I have a bunch of kids. My youngest are two years old and four years old.

I see how they learn, it's the same way all kids learn: by trying and failing.

My four-year-old is the budding artist of the group. His medium of choice is paints.

He's got this little easel with a roll of paper that comes

down and he slaps his paints all over it, making a big mess. He tries mixing colors and making shapes.

The paintings don't always turn out the way he wants. What do you expect? He's four.

When the paintings inevitably don't work out, he pulls down a new sheet of paper and tries again. Every time he tries again, he's getting more practice. It doesn't always work out, but he's learning.

This is how he learns by failure.

What kind of parent would I be if my precious little darling tried to paint a purple brontosaurus going down a waterslide and when he messed up, I yelled at him, "What are you, stupid? How could a purple brontosaurus have legs that big and a tail that small!? There's no room for terrible painters like you in this family!"

I wouldn't be a very good parent.

He is learning by failure and I should be helping him learn. I'm not going to "teach him a lesson" and it's not going to make him try hard. He's probably going to drop his paints then run to his bedroom to cry and piss his pants.

If you're a manager and you yell at someone on your team like that, they probably won't drop their TPS reports and go run into the next room crying, but they will feel like it (side note: you shouldn't be surprised if they do - one of my big revelations in my first job as a manager was how often people cried).

Don't make your teammates feel like this when they fail. People learn by failure.

My two-year-old also learns by failure. He's potty training and sometimes he doesn't make it into the potty.

What does he do when the inevitable accident occurs?

He wipes it up and tries again next time. Each time is more practice, each time he gets better. That's how potty-training works, that's how all training works.

Now what if my two-year-old had a whoopsie-daisy when he was aiming and my four-year-old pulled me aside and said, "Look at this kid, he can't even go pee-pee in the potty. He'll never be your favorite son. He can't make VP with aim like that."

As a parent, I would need to shut that down.

That's toxic conversation and I can't let that take place in my family. I would have to tell big brother that he can't talk about little brother like that, or it will stunt his growth. They both need to know that isn't ok.

As a decent and reasonable manager, you can't talk to your people negatively when they fail and you can't let anyone else talk about your people like that, either. It will stunt the growth of your people just like it stunts the growth of a potty-training two-year-old when he hears it from his four-year-old brother.

Now, this is the same four-year-old brother that tried (more than once) to pee into a garden hose *while it was running,* so maybe he's not the best person to take advice from.

Still, even in those situations, I have to handle it like a decent and reasonable human being. When I see him holding a garden hose in one hand and pushing his pants down with the other, I can scream at him, embarrass him in front his brothers, and write his name on a secret list that says he'll never make upper management, or I can say, "I appreciate you thinking outside the box and trying something new, but I don't think your latest idea is the best course of action. It's ok that you tried something new, but let's try the toilet next time."

By the same token, if one of my employees tries to be funny in a presentation to a bunch of executives and the executives don't find it funny, I have a choice on how to handle it. I could yell at my employee in the meeting (or make passive aggressive comments) to "teach them a lesson" and let everyone in the room know that I wasn't on board with that approach and then yell at them and call them stupid in front of their co-workers when we get back to our floor and tell them "you'll never make it to management if you try things like that!"

Or...

Maybe I could just withhold remarks in the moment. I could let it all play out, see how it goes and think about it a little bit. When we get back to our floor, I could pull them into a room for a quiet one on one conversation and ask them what their thought process was for their approach and how they thought it went.

It's possible they'll already realize it wasn't the best approach.

If not, I could calmly let them know that I didn't think it was appropriate for the audience and tell them that I don't think they should try that approach with that group again next time. Maybe I even ask them for a full preview before the next one.

Trust me, they'll get the point. They've learned through failure.

We all do.

For some reason, we are naturally more accepting of learning through failure when people are younger.

Think back to high school English class. If you left a dangling modifier on your paper, what would happen? Most likely, your teacher would write a red mark and maybe a little explanation to try to teach you the correct way to handle it. They would act like a decent and reasonable human being. They wouldn't tell you it was idiotic and say you could never be president.

You learned through failure.

In college calculus, if you missed your integration variable, did your professor try to make an example out of you in front of the whole class and tell you you'd never graduate because you made a mistake like that?

No, they would point out the mistake and try to help you understand it better so you could learn.

If they would have just berated you and embarrassed you, they wouldn't have helped you learn and grow and become a successful person, they would have just taught you to fear feedback, which is not a healthy way for anyone to work and makes it nearly impossible to learn.

People learn through failure.

It's natural at all ages.

But when we're done with college and enter the workplace, for some reason people think it's time to be a "professional adult" and you can't fail any more. If you ask the wrong question of a VP, you get labelled a low-potential loser. Suddenly, you're never allowed to go to meetings with a VP ever again.

How does that help? That's a cowardly move for a manager. It's them saying "I can't develop or support my people, so I'm just going to shove them in a corner until they quit or I retire."

You have to let people learn through failure, even as adults.

This is an area that the blue-collar world handles way better than the white-collar world.

If you're a mechanic and you over-tighten a bolt, you don't get banished from ever working on cars again. Ever watch a drywall crew? They make mistakes all the time, then they go right back and fix them - no one looks at their gaffes as "career-limiting moves." Painters are the same way, and after years or decades of failing and learning, they become masters.

I've failed plenty (heck, I could write a ten-book series on that), everyone has, even you.

Think about how your manager reacted when you failed. Think about how it made you feel.

If they handled it like a dick, it probably didn't make you feel great or want to work harder. On top of that, you were probably too preoccupied with what a dick your manager was being to ever really think through the important things that happened and what you could learn from it.

If your manager was a decent and reasonable human being, they probably didn't make you feel terrible. They probably helped you learn from the process and become a better worker, maybe even a better person, definitely a better-informed person.

To manage like a decent and reasonable human being, you have to take the time for calm, rational helpful discussions.

It's not easy to give direct, helpful feedback. It can be awkward, but I promise you'll survive it.

One of the hardest performance reviews I ever had to give went to someone who got a "Meets Expectations" rating (whatever your company calls it, this is the solid middle rating that almost everyone gets).

This was a person who just got a promotion after earning an "Exceeds Expectations" rating (whatever your company calls it, this is the higher rating that HR makes it extremely difficult to get) the previous year.

I take performance reviews very seriously because I believe getting 360 feedback and helping people find their blind spots and room for improvement is a critical part of helping them succeed and improve (I know I've grown a lot because people gave me that feedback... it didn't always come in a decent and reasonable manner, but that's another topic).

So I give this guy his review and let him know he had a good year and all that and I talk about one specific tiny area he could work on. It was something that he wasn't terrible at, but just didn't always focus on consistently doing well. Multiple people, including me, all felt it was something he could improve on.

Now, this guy was a classic Type A overachiever who did a really good job and produced quality work. He couldn't handle hearing that something wasn't perfect.

"No, no," I tried (unsuccessfully) to reassure him, "this isn't a big deal - it's just a piece of helpful feedback for something that you're solid at, but could do even better if you paid a little more attention to."

My comments didn't help. The guy then believed he

was downgraded because of this and would have earned a higher rating if he hadn't been (unfairly in his eyes) given this feedback (which everyone who'd ever met him for more than II seconds would say was spot on).

Still, he was upset.

I was a little baffled. This was a persistent (though not egregious) behavior. This guy wasn't from the Participation Trophy Generation, either. It felt like he had no idea this was an issue and none of his previous managers had ever bothered to tell them.

He went from upset to angry.

This is where I could have waffled, I could have softened the message and tried to placate him, I could have even (as he suggested) changed the wording in his review (which was an odd request since this feedback wasn't even documented in his official review, it was just something I told him to try to help).

I didn't.

It may have made me feel like a nice person or a helpful friend if I had done those things, but I wouldn't have been a decent and reasonable person. I would have been robbing him of the ability to improve if I didn't stand firm on the feedback. If I waffled, it would have given him a chance to dismiss the feedback and he wouldn't have been able to grow from it.

So I sat there and listened to his complaining and then calmly reiterated that this was the feedback he received. Even if he didn't agree with it, this was how others saw him.

The meeting ended with him storming out of the

room, despite receiving a solid performance review (a year after I promoted him).

It was not easy at all (remember, I warned that managing like a decent and reasonable human being isn't easy), but I am so glad I did it.

It wasn't long until this person moved to a new department. It had nothing to do with the feedback, it was the next step in his career. He was later promoted in his new area. I truly believe that he would not have been promoted if he hadn't worked on the feedback that I took such great grief to share with him.

Yes, he absolutely worked his ass off to get it, but lots of people work their ass off, pump out great work, and still miss out on promotions because they have a small thing they need to work on and no one is decent and reasonable enough to tell them about it.

This is why it's important for people like you to step up, do the hard things, and manage like a decent and reasonable human being. You don't do it because it's fun or easy, you do it because it's the right thing to do and it helps other people.

12

ADMIT PROBLEMS

I'm a competitive guy.

To a fault.

I'm not as bad as I used to be (because decent and reasonable people - and therapists - helped me understand this), but I still want to win and be right at everything.

It's just who I am.

I'm aware that this is a fault of mine (it's one of many, as luck would have it), but I'm working on improving it. When I think about self-improvement, I reflect back on my past and think of cringey stories where I was able to learn some lessons.

When I was a coder, I wanted to be the best coder around (in my younger days, when I wasn't as self-aware of my over-competitiveness as I am now, I may have added that I actually *was* the best - but since I've matured, I won't).

In college, I would rush down to the computer lab as

soon as I got a coding assignment. I'd hurry to finish my assignments, but when I was done, I was never *done*. After I had a perfectly-fine algorithm that met all the criteria of the assignment, I'd spend hours in the lab trying to get them to run faster. They didn't *need* to be faster, I just wanted them to be faster (plus, these two other jerks were always trying to make faster algorithms and I just *had to* beat them).

I was the same way at work. I would jump whenever a coding assignment came up with an algorithm in it. I'd hone the bejesus out of the damn thing trying to shave off precious hundredths of a millisecond (because if a million people ran it a billion times, you might start to save a minute or two over the course of a decade).

One time, I specifically remember how proud of myself I was to break some meaningless numeric speed barrier for no reason on an algorithm. Certainly, no one else on the team, nay, no one else in the company... maybe even no one else in *the world*, could possibly make it run faster (not that it was noticeable because it fired in like 0.0022 seconds, but I just had to get it to 0.0020).

I was so enamored with my meaningless accomplishment that I had to rush it into production and whisk myself away to the nearest bar for a well-deserved refreshment.

After enjoying an unnecessary number of alcoholic beverages (and, no doubt, entertaining everyone in the bar with my positively *hilarious* liquid wit), I went home for some hard-earned sleep.

For some reason, I was late to work the following morning. People noticed because they had been looking for me all morning. There was something wrong with the program and no one could figure it out.

"No one made any updates all week," they said.

At the risk of dating myself, this was a time when change logs were... "fluid" and... maybe... I didn't always manually update them when I published my code changes.

In fact, I'm quite certain that I didn't update the change log when I published this particular code change (I also apparently didn't change the call to the algorithm that now needed a new parameter after I rewrote it). It looked to everyone else like there hadn't been any changes, like the program just up and stopped working for no reason on the same day Bruce showed up late and hungover.

So what did I do?

Did I sheepishly raise my hand and admit, "Sorry guys, that was me. I'm really sorry, but I think I can fix it."?

Heck.

No.

I put on the dumbest looking face I could muster (which I'm sure fooled no one), scratched my head with a frown, and said, "Well that's odd. You know how those darn computers are though - always mixing up ones and zeros. Why don't I go see if I can figure out what's going on."

I scurried back to my desk, popped a couple Advil, and quickly fixed my stupid mistake. Then I actually ran a couple tests to make sure it worked before publishing the fix.

I peeked around the cube farm and made random

comments like "well that's odd" loud enough for everyone to hear. Then I went back to my manager's office and said, "Well shucks, boss, I can't see anything wrong - it seems to be working just fine now."

My dumbass act fooled precisely no one, but it saved me the embarrassment of admitting I was wrong.

Looking back, the only question I can ask my young self is: "So what?"

It was terrible and cowardly of me.

It was not a decent and reasonable thing to do.

Forget about ethics and character building (that stuff is obvious and it doesn't deter anyone), think about what I robbed my team of. I robbed them of a learning opportunity, I robbed them of the chance to say, "oh I see what you did there and how you fixed it and now I understand more and I'm a better developer" (I also robbed myself of a chance to show them my brilliant fast new algorithm, but that's probably lower on the totem pole of importance).

Worst of all, I robbed our team of the ability to connect in a different way through a shared learning experience. I robbed myself of a chance to practice vulnerability and I robbed the team of a chance to practice empathy.

My stupid algorithm was 0.0002 seconds faster, but our team was worse off because of *how* I fixed that problem (which, of course, I created).

I'm not the only one, though.

Years later (when change logs were more sophisticated) I worked on a software team where something mysteriously stopped working and no one on the team fessed up to it (or had the decency to at least go fix it behind everyone's back and then play dumb about it). No, this time, it was really messed up.

After it was fixed, my boss arranged for me to get temporary super-admin access to all the systems to investigate. I poked through all the logs it became clear that someone actually left a very obvious trail of the mistakes they'd made (including screenshots of their mistake saved to their desktop showing their id logged in... to this day, I can't believe that part).

I reported it all back to my boss and the guy got in a lot of trouble. A *lot*.

This guy didn't admit his mistake... just like I didn't admit my mistake.

Both of us were afraid of the consequences and because we were afraid of the consequences, we took actions of self-preservation and our teams suffered.

How would things have been different if we didn't fear the consequences? What if we had decent and reasonable managers who created an environment where it was totally safe - or even encouraged - to admit mistakes so everyone could learn?

What if we felt confident saying, "Sorry boss, I screwed up - this was what happened" without fear of backlash from our manager?

Our teams would have been able to learn from our mistakes. Ironically, in my story, I got to learn from my mistake, but no one else did and that was actually pretty selfish of me. If everyone could have learned a little more, who knows what kind of impact it could have had on their personal growth and on the company as a whole?

Knowledge builds on knowledge. If someone on my team would have been able to learn from my mistake, it could have set them down a path of learning more and more. Who knows what they may have come up with if they'd been able to learn from my dumbassery back then? I may have unintentionally short-circuited a cure for cancer with my fear of consequences for a stupid mistake!

If I had a manager with a history of handling those failures like a decent and reasonable human being, if I had already seen my manager turn someone's failure into a learning opportunity and handle them with dignity and class, well, things could have been wildly different - they could have been better for everyone involved.

If you won't admit mistakes and you create a culture where no one else on the team will admit mistakes, there's going to be a lot of missed opportunities for growth and a lot of wasted resources and energy. If you can't extend grace and accept mistakes when people admit them, if you're going to write someone's name on the do-not-promote list every time they screw up, you won't have a healthy work environment.

Admit your mistakes and make sure your team knows they can do the same.

13

FIRE PEOPLE HUMANELY

I f you manage people long enough, you will eventually have to fire someone.

The odds approach 100% every day you are on the job - be ready for it.

I know you're a great manager with great people at a great company, but really, you can still find yourself in this situation. A lot of times, it isn't based on the performance of the employee or the manager, it's simply the harsh reality of the business world.

When you eventually find yourself in this unenviable position, I beg you: handle it like a decent and reasonable human being.

Even if they're a spiteful person who brought it all on themselves: handle it like a decent and reasonable human being.

Even if the person sitting across the table is a total POS who showed up to work every day with the sole intention to make you and everyone else at the entire company miserable and they kick puppies, brag pretentiously about never watching tv, and sign you up for their multi-level marketing schemes even when you ask them not to, still: handle it like a decent and reasonable human being.

You want to make the world a better place by not being one of the managers that smirks about letting someone loose or worse yet, makes it a point to let them know! Be a decent and reasonable human being through this process - you owe at least that to them because you took on the mantle of leadership.

It's hard to do, even if you have the best intentions. There's a lot more wrong ways than right ways to handle these situations.

Really, though, this is where you step back, take a deep breath, and be as nice and empathetic as you possibly can.

Don't make it awkward, just be yourself and act like a friend.

Don't be combative or try to make a point, they should already get the point by now.

Don't blame anything on anyone, it doesn't matter.

Be forthright.

Listen.

Answer questions as truthfully as you can.

HR will probably have a lot of input on what you can't say. Do your best to honor that and still help the person understand what's going on.

You owe that to them.

You really do.

And you owe it to the world. When you take on the

responsibility of managing a team, you take on a responsibility to the company, and the world, to not be a dick.

Someday, you may have to do mass layoffs, too. Don't just ignore everyone, pretending you didn't get their emails and acting like you got a phone call anytime someone spots you, until they're fired (that's being a dick).

I've been around too many instances where managers just check out. They hide from their people. They ignore the questions. And then one day, everyone gets called into a room and they're told they've received their last paycheck.

That's not a decent and reasonable way to handle things.

HR will tell you that you can't tell your people what is coming. The Legal department will be very clear on that as well.

You can't just ignore what they tell you, either (I know it's really tempting, though).

But, as a decent and reasonable person, you've been using your wisdom and experience to understand the harsh realities of the business world, right? You've been letting your people know that they should always have a backup plan in case something like this happens, rights?

Good, because now is the time to remind them that they should have a backup plan.

PART III

FINAL NOTES

14

DON'T BE A DICK

Being a manager is a daunting task that can intimidate first-timers and veterans alike.

There's a lot of philosophy and maxims and rules you can follow to be a good manager.

But if you ever forget them all, just remember the one golden rule.

Don't be a dick.

Show up every day with an attitude of decency, show up striving to be reasonable. Help your team do great things and make their success (not building your empire or getting a promotion) your ultimate goal.

I've been blessed to have some amazing managers, people who truly inspired me to be better. They helped me see my flaws and shortcomings without shaming me or berating me or even using sarcasm (which tends to be my personal go-to... I'm working on that, though).

Everything in this book is something I learned

because a decent and reasonable person helped me understand it by setting a great example.

I hope you find the courage to do the same for others.

BOOK BRUCE!

Help the leaders at your organization manage like decent and reasonable human beings!

Bruce Wolf, who's delighted audiences on six continents, speaks to organizations like yours!

He's learned a lifetime of lessons from organizations ranging from Fortune 50 and Private 100 to dot coms and startups. He's worked for global niche leaders and regional chains as well as small businesses and franchisees. He's worked in financial services, marketing, manufacturing, retail, publishing, technology, volunteer, secular, education, and more.

Along the way, no matter the size, location, or industry a company is in, he's seen leaders make the same mistakes over and over again - he's seen enough to become an expert on how to ruin your company.

That's why he started HowToRuinYourCompany.com - his talks help leaders avoid the mistakes everyone else is making!

For inquiries about speaking engagements (including keynotes, panel moderation, emceeing, and more), contact: Bookings@HowToRuinYourCompany.com.

For more information, see http://www. HowToRuinYourCompany.com.

SIGN UP FOR OUR MAILING LIST!

Did you find this book interesting? Are you a decent and reasonable human being?

Want to learn more about other books when they come out, new talks on similar topics, and generally interesting stuff?

Our mailing list might be right for you...

Do you also want to be a part of a mailing list that will *never* (*ever*) sell your email or spam you every other day with nonsense (trust me, we hate that stuff, too)?

Then, our mailing list *is* right for you!

Sign up at:

HowToRuinYourCompany.com/NewsletterSignup

ABOUT THE AUTHOR

A technologist and strategist, Bruce Wolf has built his career at some of the most recognizable companies in the world.

Working for organizations ranging from Fortune 50 and Private 100 to dot coms and startups, from global niche leaders and regional chains to small businesses and franchisees, in industries including financial services, marketing, manufacturing, retail, publishing, technology, volunteer, secular, education, and more, have taught him a lot about business, leadership, and about people in general.

He learned that no matter the size, location, or industry a company is in, he's seen leaders make the same mistakes over and over again - it's been enough material to become an expert on how to ruin your company.

That's why he started HowToRuinYourCompany.com - his talks help leaders avoid the mistakes everyone else is making!

He shares his lessons through his books as well as through his speaking engagements and unique leadership workshops, which have entertained and educated business leaders on six continents.

He also likes to swap business stories and connect with people. You can drop him a line at: Bruce@HowTo-RuinYourCompany.com.